Contents

Foreword

The National Curriculum lies at the heart of our policies to raise standards. It sets out a clear, full and statutory entitlement to learning for all pupils. It determines the content of what will be taught, and sets attainment targets for learning. It also determines how performance will be assessed and reported. An effective National Curriculum therefore gives teachers, pupils, parents, employers and their wider community a clear and shared understanding of the skills and knowledge that young people will gain at school. It allows schools to meet the individual learning needs of pupils and to develop a distinctive character and ethos rooted in their local communities. And it provides a framework within which all partners in education can support young people on the road to further learning.

Getting the National Curriculum right presents difficult choices and balances. It must be robust enough to define and defend the core of knowledge and cultural experience which is the entitlement of every pupil, and at the same time flexible enough to give teachers the scope to build their teaching around it in ways which will enhance its delivery to their pupils.

The focus of this National Curriculum, together with the wider school curriculum, is therefore to ensure that pupils develop from an early age the essential literacy and numeracy skills they need to learn; to provide them with a guaranteed, full and rounded entitlement to learning; to foster their creativity; and to give teachers discretion to find the best ways to inspire in their pupils a joy and commitment to learning that will last a lifetime.

An entitlement to learning must be an entitlement for all pupils. This National Curriculum includes for the first time a detailed, overarching statement on inclusion which makes clear the principles schools must follow in their teaching right across the curriculum, to ensure that all pupils have the chance to succeed, whatever their individual needs and the potential barriers to their learning may be.

Equality of opportunity is one of a broad set of common values and purposes which underpin the school curriculum and the work of schools. These also include a commitment to valuing ourselves, our families and other relationships, the wider groups to which we belong, the diversity in our society and the environment in which we live. Until now, ours was one of the few national curricula not to have a statement of rationale setting out the fundamental principles underlying the curriculum. The handbooks for primary and secondary teachers include for the first time such a statement.

This is also the first National Curriculum in England to include citizenship, from September 2002, as part of the statutory curriculum for secondary schools. Education in citizenship and democracy will provide coherence in the way in which all pupils are helped to develop a full understanding of their roles and responsibilities as citizens in a modern democracy. It will play an important role, alongside other aspects of the curriculum and school life, in helping pupils to deal with difficult moral and social questions that arise in their lives and in society. The handbooks also provide for the first time a national framework for the teaching of personal, social and health education. Both elements reflect the fact that education is also about helping pupils to develop the knowledge, skills and understanding they need to live confident, healthy, independent lives, as individuals, parents, workers and members of society.

Rt Hon David Blunkett
Secretary of State for Education
and Employment

Sir William Stubbs
Chairman, Qualifications
and Curriculum Authority

About this booklet

This booklet:

- sets out the legal requirements of the National Curriculum in England for English
- provides information to help teachers implement English in their schools.

It has been written for coordinators, subject leaders and those who teach English, and is one of a series of separate booklets for each National Curriculum subject.

The National Curriculum for pupils aged five to 11 is set out in the handbook for primary teachers. The National Curriculum for pupils aged 11 to 16 is set out in the handbook for secondary teachers.

All these publications, and materials that support the teaching, learning and assessment of English, can be found on the National Curriculum web site at www.nc.uk.net.

About English in the National Curriculum

The structure of the National Curriculum

The programmes of study[1] set out what pupils should be taught, and the attainment targets set out the expected standards of pupils' performance. It is for schools to choose how they organise their school curriculum to include the programmes of study for English.

The programmes of study

The programmes of study set out what pupils should be taught in English at key stages 1, 2, 3 and 4 and provide the basis for planning schemes of work. When planning, schools should also consider the general teaching requirements for inclusion, use of language and use of information and communication technology that apply across the programmes of study.

At each key stage, the requirements cover speaking and listening, reading and writing. Some aspects of each are distinctive, but since language development depends on their interrelatedness, teaching needs to build on the links between them. In particular, there are strong connections between the standard English, language variation and language structure paragraphs in the different sections of the programme of study. Taken together, these provide a coherent basis for language study.

The **Knowledge, skills and understanding** have been developed alongside the relevant parts of the range outlined in **Breadth of study**. Strong links have been made, so that planning can be based on both the range of texts and activities to be provided and the skills and understanding to be developed.

Teaching should ensure that work in speaking and listening, reading and writing is integrated.

The National Literacy Strategy *Framework for teaching* offers detailed guidance on planning and implementing the programmes of study for reading and writing for pupils aged five to 11. The detailed objectives in the *Framework* cover the relevant programmes of study in English. Some aspects of speaking and listening can also be integrated into this teaching. Guidance on planning and progression in speaking and listening can be found in *Teaching speaking and listening at key stages 1 and 2* (QCA, 1999).

Schools may find the DfEE/QCA exemplar scheme of work for key stage 3 helpful to show how the programme of study and attainment targets can be translated into practical, manageable teaching plans.

[1] The Education Act 1996, section 353b, defines a programme of study as the 'matters, skills and processes' that should be taught to pupils of different abilities and maturities during the key stage.

Attainment targets and level descriptions

The attainment targets for English set out the 'knowledge, skills and understanding that pupils of different abilities and maturities are expected to have by the end of each key stage'[2]. Attainment targets consist of eight level descriptions of increasing difficulty, plus a description for exceptional performance above level 8. Each level description describes the types and range of performance that pupils working at that level should characteristically demonstrate.

The level descriptions in English indicate progression in the attainment targets for speaking and listening, reading and writing.

The level descriptions provide the basis for making judgements about pupils' performance at the end of key stages 1, 2 and 3. At key stage 4, national qualifications are the main means of assessing attainment in English.

Range of levels within which the great majority of pupils are expected to work		Expected attainment for the majority of pupils at the end of the key stage	
Key stage 1	1–3	at age 7	2
Key stage 2	2–5	at age 11	4
Key stage 3	3–7	at age 14	5/6

Assessing attainment at the end of a key stage

Each level is a broad band of attainment and may be achieved in a variety of ways, taking account of pupils' strengths and weaknesses. Evidence for the achievement of a level can be drawn from the range of a pupil's work in English during a year, to inform teacher assessment at the end of a key stage.

In deciding on a pupil's level of attainment at the end of a key stage, teachers should judge which description best fits the pupil's performance. When doing so, each description should be considered alongside descriptions for adjacent levels.

Arrangements for statutory assessment at the end of each key stage are set out in detail in QCA's annual booklets about assessment and reporting arrangements.

[2] As defined by the Education Act 1996, section 353a.

Learning across the National Curriculum

The importance of English to pupils' education is set out on page 14. The handbooks for primary and secondary teachers also set out in general terms how the National Curriculum can promote learning across the curriculum in a number of areas such as spiritual, moral, social and cultural development, key skills and thinking skills. The examples below indicate specific ways in which the teaching of English can contribute to learning across the curriculum.

Promoting pupils' spiritual, moral, social and cultural development through English

For example, English provides opportunities to promote:
- *spiritual development*, through helping pupils represent, explore and reflect on their own and others' inner life in drama and the discussion of texts and ideas
- *moral development*, through exploring questions of right and wrong, values and conflict between values in their reading of fiction and non-fiction, in their discussions and in drama
- *social development*, through helping pupils collaborate with others to create or present devised or scripted drama and to take account of the needs of the audience and the effects they wish to achieve when adapting their speech and writing, and through reading, reviewing and discussing texts that present issues and relationships between groups and between the individual and society in different historical periods and cultures
- *cultural development*, through helping pupils explore and reflect on the way that cultures are represented in their stories and poems, through introducing pupils to the English literary heritage, and through learning about language variation in English and how language relates to national, regional and cultural identities.

Promoting key skills through English

For example, English provides opportunities for pupils to develop the key skills:
- *communication*, through work at all key stages on speaking and listening, reading and writing. The programme of study for key stages 3 and 4 specifically includes components of the key skill of communication. It incorporates:
  - contributing to a discussion, making clear and relevant contributions and listening and responding appropriately
  - giving a short talk with a clear structure, speaking clearly and illustrating main points
  - selecting, reading and summarising information, identifying the main points and lines of reasoning
  - writing that presents relevant information in a structured way and is technically accurate
- *IT*, through opportunities to work on screen and with a variety of media and to communicate using e-mail and the internet
- *working with others*, through collaborative group work and drama
- *improving own learning and performance*, through the process of drafting writing and of reflecting on what has been spoken, performed, read and written
- *problem solving*, through group work and drama.

Promoting other aspects of the curriculum

English can play a part in promoting citizenship and thinking skills through, for example:

- reading, viewing and discussing texts which present issues and relationships between groups and between the individual and society in different historical periods and cultures
- learning about the social, historical, political and cultural contexts which shape and influence the texts pupils read and view
- developing pupils' ability to put their point of view, question, argue and discuss, adapting what they say to their audience and the effect they wish to achieve
- evaluating critically what they hear, read and view, with attention to explicit and implied meanings, bias and objectivity, and fact and opinion
- becoming competent users of spoken and written standard English to enable pupils to participate fully in the wider world beyond school, in public life, and in decision making.

The programmes of study for English

A common structure and design for all subjects

The programmes of study

The National Curriculum programmes of study have been given a common structure and a common design.

In each subject, at each key stage, the main column **1** contains the programme of study, which sets out two sorts of requirements:

- **Knowledge, skills and understanding 2** – what has to be taught in the subject during the key stage
- **Breadth of study 3** – the contexts, activities, areas of study and range of experiences through which the **Knowledge, skills and understanding** should be taught.

Schools are not required by law to teach the content in grey type. This includes the examples in the main column **4** [printed inside square brackets], all text in the margins **5** and information and examples in the inclusion statement. In the programmes of study *italic type* is used to emphasise options, where schools and teachers can choose between requirements.

The programmes of study for English, mathematics and science

The programmes of study for English and science contain sections that correspond directly to the attainment targets for each subject. In mathematics this one-to-one correspondence does not hold for all key stages – see the mathematics programme of study for more information. In English, the three sections of the programme of study each contain **Breadth of study** requirements. In mathematics and science there is a single, separate set of **Breadth of study** requirements for each key stage.

The programmes of study in the non-core foundation subjects

In these subjects (except for citizenship) the programme of study simply contains two sets of requirements – **Knowledge, skills and understanding** and **Breadth of study**. The programmes of study for citizenship contain no **Breadth of study** requirements.

Information in the margins

At the start of each key stage, the margin begins with a summary of the main things that pupils will learn during the key stage. The margins also contain four other types of non-statutory information:

- notes giving key information that should be taken into account when teaching the subject
- notes giving definitions of words and phrases in the programmes of study
- suggested opportunities for pupils to use information and communication technology (ICT) as they learn the subject
- some key links with other subjects indicating connections between teaching requirements, and suggesting how a requirement in one subject can build on the requirements in another in the same key stage.

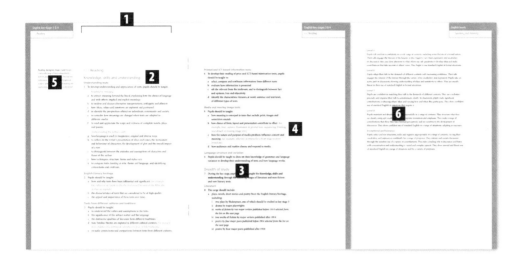

The referencing system

References work as follows:

A reference in …	… reads …	… and means …
Physical education key stage 2	**11a, 11b → links to other subjects** These requirements build on Gg/2c.	Physical education key stage 2, requirements 11a and 11b build on geography (key stage 2), paragraph 2, requirement c.
Art and design key stage 1	**4a → links to other subjects** This requirement builds on Ma3/2a, 2c, 2d.	Art and design key stage 1, requirement 4a builds on mathematics (key stage 1), Ma3 Shape, space and measures, paragraph 2, requirements a, c and d.
Citizenship key stage 3	**1a → links to other subjects** This requirement builds on Hi/10, 13.	Citizenship key stage 3, requirement 1a builds on history (key stage 3) paragraphs 10 and 13.

The attainment targets

The attainment targets **6** are at the end of this booklet. They can be read alongside the programmes of study by folding out the flaps.

I am going to the fair
will I leave my tummy
there
floating in the air
on the roller coaster
with my flying hair

The importance of English
English is a vital way of communicating
in school, in public life and internationally.
Literature in English is rich and influential,
reflecting the experience of people from
many countries and times.
In studying English pupils develop skills
in speaking, listening, reading and writing.
It enables them to express themselves
creatively and imaginatively and to
communicate with others effectively.
Pupils learn to become enthusiastic
and critical readers of stories, poetry and
drama as well as non-fiction and media texts.
The study of English helps pupils understand
how language works by looking at its
patterns, structures and origins. Using
this knowledge pupils can choose and
adapt what they say and write in
different situations.

The value of English in the curriculum? What can I say?
Without English, nothing. And without good English,
nothing very well.
Anne Fine, Author

English is the language of the future, the language of the
computer. English is the most important tool you'll ever
need, no matter what career you choose. You have the right
to English. Make it your right!
Benjamin Zephaniah, Poet, Writer, Actor, TV & Radio Presenter

A good book, studied with a good English teacher, takes you
on a journey in search of answers to the crucial questions in
life you didn't even know you wanted (or needed) to ask.
Professor Lisa Jardine, Queen Mary & Westfield College, University of London

Studying English literature at school was my first, and
probably my biggest, step towards mental freedom and
independence. It was like falling in love with life.
Ian McEwan, Novelist

Humanlife on One

The human crouches in the shadows, patiently awaiting his victim. His sharp, darting eyes watch every movement, his ears listening and alert. A fellow predator, an enemy from another pack, catches his eye. He is also watching for the same prey. They both try to reach the best spot, while simultaneously attempting to look inconspicuous. His weapon, deadly to his prey, hidden in his pouch, is ready to be whipped out at any second. A tiny movement within the hunted's safe-haven causes the hunter to become stone-still, ready to pounce when the time is right. The entry of the victim's habitat opens. A small face peeks out, clad in sunglasses and baseball cap, the face barely visible. The pitiful disguise is unsuccessful: the hunter is not discouraged. He remains perfectly still, waiting for the right moment. The prey glances around suspiciously, but assured she is not being watched, the face becomes a full body, creeping out into the open. Only now does the predator spring into action, leaping from the shadows, whipping out his camera and, before the victim can scream, "NO PHOTOS," the deed is done, the exclusive photo taken. The A-list celebrity is indeed becoming an endangered species.

Programme of study: English

Key stage 1

In English, during key stage 1 pupils learn to speak confidently and listen to what others have to say. They begin to read and write independently and with enthusiasm. They use language to explore their own experiences and imaginary worlds.

Speaking and listening: during key stage 1 pupils learn to speak clearly, thinking about the needs of their listeners. They work in small groups and as a class, joining in discussions and making relevant points. They also learn how to listen carefully to what other people are saying, so that they can remember the main points. They learn to use language in imaginative ways and express their ideas and feelings when working in role and in drama activities.

Building on the early learning goals
Pupils' prior experience of speaking and listening includes:

- using language to imagine and recreate roles and experiences
- attentive listening and response
- interacting with others in play and to get things done.

Teaching should ensure that work in **speaking and listening**, **reading** and **writing** is integrated.

En1 Speaking and listening

Knowledge, skills and understanding

Speaking

1   To speak clearly, fluently and confidently to different people, pupils should be taught to:
   a   speak with clear diction and appropriate intonation
   b   choose words with precision
   c   organise what they say
   d   focus on the main point(s)
   e   include relevant detail
   f   take into account the needs of their listeners.

Listening

2   To listen, understand and respond to others, pupils should be taught to:
   a   sustain concentration
   b   remember specific points that interest them
   c   make relevant comments
   d   listen to others' reactions
   e   ask questions to clarify their understanding
   f   identify and respond to sound patterns in language [for example, alliteration, rhyme, word play].

Group discussion and interaction

3   To join in as members of a group, pupils should be taught to:
   a   take turns in speaking
   b   relate their contributions to what has gone on before
   c   take different views into account
   d   extend their ideas in the light of discussion
   e   give reasons for opinions and actions.

Drama

4   To participate in a range of drama activities, pupils should be taught to:
   a   use language and actions to explore and convey situations, characters and emotions
   b   create and sustain roles individually and when working with others
   c   comment constructively on drama they have watched or in which they have taken part.

Standard English

5 Pupils should be introduced to some of the main features of spoken standard English and be taught to use them.

Language variation

6 Pupils should be taught about how speech varies:

a in different circumstances [for example, to reflect on how their speech changes in more formal situations]

b to take account of different listeners [for example, adapting what they say when speaking to people they do not know].

Breadth of study

7 During the key stage, pupils should be taught the **Knowledge, skills and understanding** through the following range of activities, contexts and purposes.

Speaking

8 The range should include:

a telling stories, real and imagined

b reading aloud and reciting

c describing events and experiences

d speaking to different people, including friends, the class, teachers and other adults.

Listening

9 The range should include opportunities for pupils to listen to:

a each other

b adults giving detailed explanations and presentations [for example, describing how a model works, reading aloud]

c recordings [for example, radio, television].

Group discussion and interaction

10 The range of purposes should include:

a making plans and investigating

b sharing ideas and experiences

c commenting and reporting.

Drama activities

11 The range should include:

a working in role

b presenting drama and stories to others [for example, telling a story through tableaux or using a narrator]

c responding to performances.

Note on standard English

The paragraphs on **standard English**, **language variation**, **language structure** and **language structure and variation** in **speaking and listening**, **reading** and **writing** provide a coherent basis for language study.

Note for 5

When teaching **standard English** it is helpful to bear in mind the most common non-standard usages in England:

- subject–verb agreements (they was)
- formation of past tense (have fell, I done)
- formation of negatives (ain't).

Reading: during key stage 1 pupils' interest and pleasure in reading is developed as they learn to read confidently and independently. They focus on words and sentences and how they fit into whole texts. They work out the meaning of straightforward texts and say why they like them or do not like them.

The programme of study for English and the National Literacy Strategy *Framework for teaching* are closely related. The *Framework* provides a detailed basis for implementing the statutory requirements of the programmes of study for **reading** and **writing**.

Building on the early learning goals
Pupils' prior experience of literacy includes:
- knowledge of initial and final sounds and short vowel sounds in words
- stories, poems and other texts
- recognition of some familiar words.

Note for 2a
Organisational features in CD-ROMs and web pages include icons, hotlinks and menus.

En2 Reading

Knowledge, skills and understanding

Reading strategies

1 To read with fluency, accuracy, understanding and enjoyment, pupils should be taught to use a range of strategies to make sense of what they read. They should be taught to:

Phonemic awareness and phonic knowledge

a hear, identify, segment and blend phonemes in words

b sound and name the letters of the alphabet

c link sound and letter patterns, exploring rhyme, alliteration and other sound patterns

d identify syllables in words

e recognise that the same sounds may have different spellings and that the same spellings may relate to different sounds

Word recognition and graphic knowledge

f read on sight high-frequency words and other familiar words

g recognise words with common spelling patterns

h recognise specific parts of words, including prefixes, suffixes, inflectional endings, plurals

Grammatical awareness

i understand how word order affects meaning

j decipher new words, and confirm or check meaning

k work out the sense of a sentence by rereading or reading ahead

Contextual understanding

l focus on meaning derived from the text as a whole

m use their knowledge of book conventions, structure, sequence and presentational devices

n draw on their background knowledge and understanding of the content.

Reading for information

2 Pupils should be taught to:

a use the organisational features of non-fiction texts, including captions, illustrations, contents, index and chapters, to find information

b understand that texts about the same topic may contain different information or present similar information in different ways

c use reference materials for different purposes.

Literature

3   To develop their understanding of fiction, poetry and drama, pupils should
    be taught to:

    a   identify and describe characters, events and settings in fiction

    b   use their knowledge of sequence and story language when they are retelling
        stories and predicting events

    c   express preferences, giving reasons

    d   learn, recite and act out stories and poems

    e   identify patterns of rhythm, rhyme and sounds in poems and their effects

    f   respond imaginatively in different ways to what they read [for example,
        using the characters from a story in drama, writing poems based on ones
        they read, showing their understanding through art or music].

Language structure and variation

4   To read texts with greater accuracy and understanding, pupils should be taught
    about the characteristics of different types of text [for example, beginnings and
    endings in stories, use of captions].

Breadth of study

5   During the key stage, pupils should be taught the **Knowledge, skills and**
    understanding through the following ranges of literature and non-fiction
    and non-literary texts.

Literature

6   The range should include:

    a   stories and poems with familiar settings and those based on imaginary
        or fantasy worlds

    b   stories, plays and poems by significant children's authors

    c   retellings of traditional folk and fairy stories

    d   stories and poems from a range of cultures

    e   stories, plays and poems with patterned and predictable language

    f   stories and poems that are challenging in terms of length or vocabulary

    g   texts where the use of language benefits from being read aloud and reread.

Non-fiction and non-literary texts

7   The range should include:

    a   print and ICT-based information texts, including those with continuous
        text and relevant illustrations

    b   dictionaries, encyclopedias and other reference materials.

Writing: during key stage 1 pupils start to enjoy writing and see the value of it. They learn to communicate meaning in narrative and non-fiction texts and spell and punctuate correctly.

The programme of study for English and the National Literacy Strategy *Framework for teaching* are closely related. The *Framework* provides a detailed basis for implementing the statutory requirements of the programmes of study for **reading** and **writing**.

Building on the early learning goals
Pupils' prior experience of literacy includes:
- differentiating between print and pictures
- the connections between speech and writing
- the symbolic nature of writing, the sounds and names of letters and how to write them.

2c → ICT opportunity
Pupils could compare print-outs from two different drafts of their own writing to check revisions and improvements.

En3 Writing

Knowledge, skills and understanding

Composition

1 Pupils should be taught to:

a use adventurous and wide-ranging vocabulary

b sequence events and recount them in appropriate detail

c put their ideas into sentences

d use a clear structure to organise their writing

e vary their writing to suit the purpose and reader

f use the texts they read as models for their own writing.

Planning and drafting

2 Working with the teacher and with others, in order to develop their writing, pupils should be taught to:

a write familiar words and attempt unfamiliar ones

b assemble and develop ideas on paper and on screen

c plan and review their writing, discussing the quality of what is written

d write extended texts, with support [for example, using the teacher as writer].

Punctuation

3 Pupils should be taught:

a how punctuation helps a reader understand what is written

b the connections between punctuation and sentence structure, intonation and emphasis

c to use capital letters, full stops, question marks and to begin to use commas.

Spelling

4 Pupils should be taught to:

Spelling strategies

a write each letter of the alphabet

b use their knowledge of sound–symbol relationships and phonological patterns [for example, consonant clusters and vowel phonemes]

c recognise and use simple spelling patterns

d write common letter strings

e spell common words

f spell words with common prefixes and inflectional endings

Checking spelling

g check the accuracy of their spelling, using word banks and dictionaries

h use their knowledge of word families and other words

i identify reasons for misspellings.

Handwriting and presentation

5   In order to develop a legible style, pupils should be taught:

Handwriting

a   how to hold a pencil/pen

b   to write from left to right and top to bottom of a page

c   to start and finish letters correctly

d   to form letters of regular size and shape

e   to put regular spaces between letters and words

f   how to form lower- and upper-case letters

g   how to join letters

Presentation

h   the importance of clear and neat presentation in order to communicate their meaning effectively.

Standard English

6   Pupils should be taught some of the grammatical features of written standard English.

Language structure

7   In composing their own texts, pupils should be taught to consider:

a   how word choice and order are crucial to meaning

b   the nature and use of nouns, verbs and pronouns

c   how ideas may be linked in sentences and how sequences of sentences fit together.

Breadth of study

8   During the key stage, pupils should be taught the **Knowledge, skills and understanding** through addressing the following ranges of purposes, readers and forms of writing.

9   The range of purposes for writing should include:

a   to communicate to others

b   to create imaginary worlds

c   to explore experience

d   to organise and explain information.

10 Pupils should be taught the value of writing for remembering and developing ideas.

11 The range of readers for writing should include teachers, other adults, children and the writers themselves.

12 The range of forms of writing should include narratives, poems, notes, lists, captions, records, messages, instructions.

Programme of study: English

Key stage 2

In English, during key stage 2 pupils learn to change the way they speak and write to suit different situations, purposes and audiences. They read a range of texts and respond to different layers of meaning in them. They explore the use of language in literary and non-literary texts and learn how language works.

Speaking and listening: during key stage 2 pupils learn how to speak in a range of contexts, adapting what they say and how they say it to the purpose and the audience. Taking varied roles in groups gives them opportunities to contribute to situations with different demands. They also learn to respond appropriately to others, thinking about what has been said and the language used.

Teaching should ensure that work in **speaking and listening**, **reading** and **writing** is integrated.

En1 Speaking and listening

Knowledge, skills and understanding

Speaking

1 To speak with confidence in a range of contexts, adapting their speech for a range of purposes and audiences, pupils should be taught to:

   a use vocabulary and syntax that enables them to communicate more complex meanings

   b gain and maintain the interest and response of different audiences [for example, by exaggeration, humour, varying pace and using persuasive language to achieve particular effects]

   c choose material that is relevant to the topic and to the listeners

   d show clear shape and organisation with an introduction and an ending

   e speak audibly and clearly, using spoken standard English in formal contexts

   f evaluate their speech and reflect on how it varies.

Listening

2 To listen, understand and respond appropriately to others, pupils should be taught to:

   a identify the gist of an account or key points in a discussion and evaluate what they hear

   b ask relevant questions to clarify, extend and follow up ideas

   c recall and re-present important features of an argument, talk, reading, radio or television programme, film

   d identify features of language used for a specific purpose [for example, to persuade, instruct or entertain]

   e respond to others appropriately, taking into account what they say.

Group discussion and interaction

3 To talk effectively as members of a group, pupils should be taught to:

   a make contributions relevant to the topic and take turns in discussion

   b vary contributions to suit the activity and purpose, including exploratory and tentative comments where ideas are being collected together, and reasoned, evaluative comments as discussion moves to conclusions or actions

   c qualify or justify what they think after listening to others' questions or accounts

   d deal politely with opposing points of view and enable discussion to move on

   e take up and sustain different roles, adapting them to suit the situation, including chair, scribe and spokesperson

f   use different ways to help the group move forward, including summarising the main points, reviewing what has been said, clarifying, drawing others in, reaching agreement, considering alternatives and anticipating consequences.

Drama

4   To participate in a wide range of drama activities and to evaluate their own and others' contributions, pupils should be taught to:

a   create, adapt and sustain different roles, individually and in groups

b   use character, action and narrative to convey story, themes, emotions, ideas in plays they devise and script

c   use dramatic techniques to explore characters and issues [for example, hot seating, flashback]

d   evaluate how they and others have contributed to the overall effectiveness of performances.

Standard English

5   Pupils should be taught the grammatical constructions that are characteristic of spoken standard English and to apply this knowledge appropriately in a range of contexts.

Language variation

6   Pupils should be taught about how language varies:

a   according to context and purpose [for example, choice of vocabulary in more formal situations]

b   between standard and dialect forms [for example, in drama, the effect of using standard or dialect forms]

c   between spoken and written forms [for example, the differences between transcribed speech, direct speech and reported speech].

Breadth of study

7   During the key stage, pupils should be taught the **Knowledge, skills and understanding** through the following range of activities, contexts and purposes.

Speaking

8   The range should include:

a   reading aloud

b   presenting to different audiences

c   extended speaking for different purposes.

Listening

9   The range should include opportunities for pupils to listen to:

a   live talks/readings/presentations

b   recordings [for example, radio, television, film]

c   others in groups.

Note on standard English
The paragraphs on **standard English**, **language variation**, **language structure** and **language structure and variation** in **speaking and listening**, **reading** and **writing** provide a coherent basis for language study.

Note for 5
When teaching **standard English** it is helpful to bear in mind the most common non-standard usages in England:

- subject–verb agreement (they was)
- formation of past tense (have fell, I done)
- formation of negatives (ain't)
- formation of adverbs (come quick)
- use of demonstrative pronouns (them books).

Group discussion and interaction

10 The range of purposes should include:

   a investigating, selecting, sorting

   b planning, predicting, exploring

   c explaining, reporting, evaluating.

Drama activities

11 The range should include:

   a improvisation and working in role

   b scripting and performing in plays

   c responding to performances.

En2 Reading

Knowledge, skills and understanding

Reading strategies

1   To read with fluency, accuracy and understanding, pupils should be taught
    to use:
    a   phonemic awareness and phonic knowledge
    b   word recognition and graphic knowledge
    c   knowledge of grammatical structures
    d   contextual understanding.

Understanding texts

2   Pupils should be taught to:
    a   use inference and deduction
    b   look for meaning beyond the literal
    c   make connections between different parts of a text [for example, how stories
        begin and end, what has been included and omitted in information writing]
    d   use their knowledge of other texts they have read.

Reading for information

3   Pupils should be taught to:
    a   scan texts to find information
    b   skim for gist and overall impression
    c   obtain specific information through detailed reading
    d   draw on different features of texts, including print, sound and image,
        to obtain meaning
    e   use organisational features and systems to find texts and information
    f   distinguish between fact and opinion [for example, by looking at the
        purpose of the text, the reliability of information]
    g   consider an argument critically.

Literature

4   To develop understanding and appreciation of literary texts, pupils should
    be taught to:
    a   recognise the choice, use and effect of figurative language, vocabulary
        and patterns of language
    b   identify different ways of constructing sentences and their effects
    c   identify how character and setting are created, and how plot, narrative
        structure and themes are developed
    d   recognise the differences between author, narrator and character
    e   evaluate ideas and themes that broaden perspectives and extend thinking
    f   consider poetic forms and their effects

Reading: during key stage 2 pupils read enthusiastically a range of materials and use their knowledge of words, sentences and texts to understand and respond to the meaning. They increase their ability to read challenging and lengthy texts independently. They reflect on the meaning of texts, analysing and discussing them with others.

The programme of study for English and the National Literacy Strategy *Framework for teaching* are closely related. The *Framework* provides a detailed basis for implementing the statutory requirements of the programmes of study for **reading** and **writing**.

Note for 3a–3e
Retrieving information on screen includes knowing how to:
- use the search and find facilities to skim and scan effectively
- use key words
- summarise information rather than print off large sections of text.

8 → ICT opportunity

Pupils could use moving image texts (for example, television, film, multimedia) to support their study of literary texts and to study how words, images and sounds are combined to convey meaning and emotion.

g express preferences and support their views by reference to texts

h respond imaginatively, drawing on the whole text and other reading

i read stories, poems and plays aloud.

Non-fiction and non-literary texts

5 To develop understanding and appreciation of non-fiction and non-literary texts, pupils should be taught to:

a identify the use and effect of specialist vocabulary

b identify words associated with reason, persuasion, argument, explanation, instruction and description

c recognise phrases and sentences that convey a formal, impersonal tone

d identify links between ideas and sentences in non-chronological writing

e understand the structural and organisational features of different types of text [for example, paragraphing, subheadings, links in hypertext]

f evaluate different formats, layouts and presentational devices [for example, tables, bullet points, icons]

g engage with challenging and demanding subject matter.

Language structure and variation

6 To read texts with greater accuracy and understanding, pupils should be taught to identify and comment on features of English at word, sentence and text level, using appropriate terminology [for example, how adjectives and adverbs contribute to overall effect, the use of varying sentence length and structure, connections between chapters or sections].

Breadth of study

7 During the key stage, pupils should be taught the **Knowledge, skills and understanding** through the following ranges of literature and non-fiction and non-literary texts.

Literature

8 The range should include:

a a range of modern fiction by significant children's authors

b long-established children's fiction

c a range of good-quality modern poetry

d classic poetry

e texts drawn from a variety of cultures and traditions

f myths, legends and traditional stories

g playscripts.

Non-fiction and non-literary texts

9   The range should include:

a   diaries, autobiographies, biographies, letters

b   print and ICT-based reference and information materials [for example, textbooks, reports, encyclopedias, handbooks, dictionaries, thesauruses, glossaries, CD-ROMs, internet]

c   newspapers, magazines, articles, leaflets, brochures, advertisements.

Writing: during key stage 2 pupils develop understanding that writing is both essential to thinking and learning, and enjoyable in its own right. They learn the main rules and conventions of written English and start to explore how the English language can be used to express meaning in different ways. They use the planning, drafting and editing process to improve their work and to sustain their fiction and non-fiction writing.

The programme of study for English and the National Literacy Strategy *Framework for teaching* are closely related. The *Framework* provides a detailed basis for implementing the statutory requirements of the programmes of study for **reading** and **writing**.

1 → ICT opportunity
Pupils could compose on screen and on paper.

Note for 2a, 2d
On screen this includes using the planning and proofing tools in a word processor (for example, thesaurus, grammar checker).

En3 Writing

Knowledge, skills and understanding

Composition

1 Pupils should be taught to:
   a choose form and content to suit a particular purpose [for example, notes to read or organise thinking, plans for action, poetry for pleasure]
   b broaden their vocabulary and use it in inventive ways
   c use language and style that are appropriate to the reader
   d use and adapt the features of a form of writing, drawing on their reading
   e use features of layout, presentation and organisation effectively.

Planning and drafting

2 To develop their writing on paper and on screen, pupils should be taught to:
   a plan – note and develop initial ideas
   b draft – develop ideas from the plan into structured written text
   c revise – change and improve the draft
   d proofread – check the draft for spelling and punctuation errors, omissions and repetitions
   e present – prepare a neat, correct and clear final copy
   f discuss and evaluate their own and others' writing.

Punctuation

3 Pupils should be taught to use punctuation marks correctly in their writing, including full stops, question and exclamation marks, commas, inverted commas, and apostrophes to mark possession and omission.

Spelling

4 Pupils should be taught:

   Spelling strategies
   a to sound out phonemes
   b to analyse words into syllables and other known words
   c to apply knowledge of spelling conventions
   d to use knowledge of common letter strings, visual patterns and analogies
   e to check their spelling using word banks, dictionaries and spellcheckers
   f to revise and build on their knowledge of words and spelling patterns

   Morphology
   g the meaning, use and spelling of common prefixes and suffixes
   h the spelling of words with inflectional endings
   i the relevance of word families, roots and origins of words
   j the use of appropriate terminology, including vowel, consonant, homophone and syllable.

Handwriting and presentation

5   Pupils should be taught to:

a   write legibly in both joined and printed styles with increasing fluency and speed

b   use different forms of handwriting for different purposes [for example, print for labelling maps or diagrams, a clear, neat hand for finished presented work, a faster script for notes].

Standard English

6   Pupils should be taught:

a   how written standard English varies in degrees of formality [for example, differences between a letter to a friend about a school trip and a report for display]

b   some of the differences between standard and non-standard English usage, including subject–verb agreements and use of prepositions.

Language structure

7   Pupils should be taught:

a   word classes and the grammatical functions of words, including nouns, verbs, adjectives, adverbs, pronouns, prepositions, conjunctions, articles

b   the features of different types of sentence, including statements, questions and commands, and how to use them [for example, imperatives in commands]

c   the grammar of complex sentences, including clauses, phrases and connectives

d   the purposes and organisational features of paragraphs, and how ideas can be linked.

Breadth of study

8   During the key stage, pupils should be taught the **Knowledge, skills and understanding** through addressing the following range of purposes, readers and forms of writing.

9   The range of purposes for writing should include:

a   to imagine and explore feelings and ideas, focusing on creative uses of language and how to interest the reader

b   to inform and explain, focusing on the subject matter and how to convey it in sufficient detail for the reader

c   to persuade, focusing on how arguments and evidence are built up and language used to convince the reader

d   to review and comment on what has been read, seen or heard, focusing on both the topic and the writer's view of it.

10 Pupils should also be taught to use writing to help their thinking, investigating, organising and learning.

Note for 9
The selection of a form for writing is closely related to the writer's purpose and the intended reader.

Note for 11

Readers could include those contacted through post, fax or e-mail.

Note for 12

Each of the forms within this range includes different text types with specific organisational and grammatical conventions.

11 The range of readers for writing should include teachers, the class, other children, adults, the wider community and imagined readers.

12 The range of forms of writing should include narratives, poems, playscripts, reports, explanations, opinions, instructions, reviews, commentaries.

Programme of study: English

Key stages 3 & 4

Teaching should ensure that work in **speaking and listening**, **reading** and **writing** is integrated.

En1 Speaking and listening

Knowledge, skills and understanding

Speaking

1 To speak fluently and appropriately in different contexts, adapting their talk for a range of purposes and audiences, including the more formal, pupils should be taught to:

   a structure their talk clearly, using markers so that their listeners can follow the line of thought

   b use illustrations, evidence and anecdote to enrich and explain their ideas

   c use gesture, tone, pace and rhetorical devices for emphasis

   d use visual aids and images to enhance communication

   e vary word choices, including technical vocabulary, and sentence structure for different audiences

   f use spoken standard English fluently in different contexts

   g evaluate the effectiveness of their speech and consider how to adapt it to a range of situations.

Listening

2 To listen, understand and respond critically to others, pupils should be taught to:

   a concentrate on and recall the main features of a talk, reading, radio or television programme

   b identify the major elements of what is being said both explicitly and implicitly

   c distinguish features of presentation where a speaker aims to explain, persuade, amuse or argue a case

   d distinguish tone, undertone, implications and other signs of a speaker's intentions

   e recognise when a speaker is being ambiguous or deliberately vague, glosses over points, uses and abuses evidence and makes unsubstantiated statements

   f ask questions and give relevant and helpful comments.

Group discussion and interaction

3 To participate effectively as members of different groups, pupils should be taught to:

   a make different types of contributions to groups, adapting their speech to their listeners and the activity

   b take different views into account and modify their own views in the light of what others say

In English, during key stage 3 pupils develop confidence in speaking and writing for public and formal purposes. They also develop their ability to evaluate the way language is used. They read classic and contemporary texts and explore social and moral issues.

In English, during key stage 4 pupils learn to use language confidently, both in their academic studies and for the world beyond school. They use and analyse complex features of language. They are keen readers who can read many kinds of text and make articulate and perceptive comments about them.

Speaking and listening: during key stages 3 and 4 pupils learn to speak and listen confidently in a wide variety of contexts. They learn to be flexible, adapting what they say and how they say it to different situations and people. When they speak formally or to people they do not know, they are articulate and fluent in their use of spoken standard English. They learn how to evaluate the contributions they, and others, have made to discussions and drama activities. They take leading and other roles in group work.

Note on standard English
The paragraphs on **standard English**, **language variation**, **language structure** and **language structure and variation** in **speaking and listening**, **reading** and **writing** provide a coherent basis for language study.

Note for 5
When teaching **standard English** it is helpful to bear in mind the most common non-standard usages in England:

- subject–verb agreement (they was)
- formation of past tense (have fell, I done)
- formation of negatives (ain't)
- formation of adverbs (come quick)
- use of demonstrative pronouns (them books)
- use of pronouns (me and him went)
- use of prepositions (out the door).

c   sift, summarise and use the most important points

d   take different roles in the organisation, planning and sustaining of groups

e   help the group to complete its tasks by varying contributions appropriately, clarifying and synthesising others' ideas, taking them forward and building on them to reach conclusions, negotiating consensus or agreeing to differ.

Drama

4   To participate in a range of drama activities and to evaluate their own and others' contributions, pupils should be taught to:

a   use a variety of dramatic techniques to explore ideas, issues, texts and meanings

b   use different ways to convey action, character, atmosphere and tension when they are scripting and performing in plays [for example, through dialogue, movement, pace]

c   appreciate how the structure and organisation of scenes and plays contribute to dramatic effect

d   evaluate critically performances of dramas that they have watched or in which they have taken part.

Standard English

5   Pupils should be taught to use the vocabulary, structures and grammar of spoken standard English fluently and accurately in informal and formal situations.

Language variation

6   Pupils should be taught about how language varies, including:

a   the importance of standard English as the language of public communication nationally and often internationally

b   current influences on spoken and written language

c   attitudes to language use

d   the differences between speech and writing

e   the vocabulary and grammar of standard English and dialectal variation

f   the development of English, including changes over time, borrowings from other languages, origins of words, and the impact of electronic communication on written language.

Breadth of study

7 During the key stage, pupils should be taught the **Knowledge, skills and understanding** through the following range of activities, contexts and purposes.

Speaking

8 The range of purposes should include:

a describing, narrating, explaining, arguing, persuading, entertaining
   and pupils should be given opportunities to make:

b extended contributions to talk in different contexts and groups

c presentations to different audiences.

Listening

9 The range should include listening to and watching:

a live talks and presentations

b recordings [for example, radio, television, film]

c discussions in which pupils respond straight away.

Group discussion and interaction

10 The range of purposes should include:

a exploring, hypothesising, debating, analysing
   and pupils should be given opportunities to:

b take different roles in groups [for example, roles in organising or leading
   discussion, supporting others, enabling focused talk].

Drama activities

11 The range should include:

a improvisation and working in role

b devising, scripting and performing in plays

c discussing and reviewing their own and others' performances.

Note for 10
Interaction may be face-to-face or by electronic means.

Reading: during key stages 3 and 4 pupils read a wide range of texts independently, both for pleasure and for study. They become enthusiastic, discriminating and responsive readers, understanding layers of meaning and appreciating what they read on a critical level.

En2 Reading

Knowledge, skills and understanding

Understanding texts

1   To develop understanding and appreciation of texts, pupils should be taught:

Reading for meaning

a   to extract meaning beyond the literal, explaining how the choice of language and style affects implied and explicit meanings

b   to analyse and discuss alternative interpretations, ambiguity and allusion

c   how ideas, values and emotions are explored and portrayed

d   to identify the perspectives offered on individuals, community and society

e   to consider how meanings are changed when texts are adapted to different media

f   to read and appreciate the scope and richness of complete novels, plays and poems

Understanding the author's craft

g   how language is used in imaginative, original and diverse ways

h   to reflect on the writer's presentation of ideas and issues, the motivation and behaviour of characters, the development of plot and the overall impact of a text

i   to distinguish between the attitudes and assumptions of characters and those of the author

j   how techniques, structure, forms and styles vary

k   to compare texts, looking at style, theme and language, and identifying connections and contrasts.

English literary heritage

2   Pupils should be taught:

a   how and why texts have been influential and significant [for example, the influence of Greek myths, the Authorised Version of the Bible, the Arthurian legends]

b   the characteristics of texts that are considered to be of high quality

c   the appeal and importance of these texts over time.

Texts from different cultures and traditions

3   Pupils should be taught:

a   to understand the values and assumptions in the texts

b   the significance of the subject matter and the language

c   the distinctive qualities of literature from different traditions

d   how familiar themes are explored in different cultural contexts [for example, how childhood is portrayed, references to oral or folk traditions]

e   to make connections and comparisons between texts from different cultures.

Printed and ICT-based information texts

4   To develop their reading of print and ICT-based information texts, pupils should be taught to:

   a   select, compare and synthesise information from different texts

   b   evaluate how information is presented

   c   sift the relevant from the irrelevant, and distinguish between fact and opinion, bias and objectivity

   d   identify the characteristic features, at word, sentence and text level, of different types of texts.

Media and moving image texts

5   Pupils should be taught:

   a   how meaning is conveyed in texts that include print, images and sometimes sounds

   b   how choice of form, layout and presentation contribute to effect [for example, font, caption, illustration in printed text, sequencing, framing, soundtrack in moving image text]

   c   how the nature and purpose of media products influence content and meaning [for example, selection of stories for a front page or news broadcast]

   d   how audiences and readers choose and respond to media.

Language structure and variation

6   Pupils should be taught to draw on their knowledge of grammar and language variation to develop their understanding of texts and how language works.

Breadth of study

7   During the key stage, pupils should be taught the **Knowledge, skills and understanding** through the following ranges of literature and non-fiction and non-literary texts.

Literature

8   The range should include:

   a   plays, novels, short stories and poetry from the English literary heritage, including:

   i   two plays by Shakespeare, one of which should be studied in key stage 3

   ii   drama by major playwrights

   iii works of fiction by two major writers published before 1914 selected from the list on page 36

   iv   two works of fiction by major writers published after 1914

   v   poetry by four major poets published before 1914 selected from the list on page 36

   vi   poetry by four major poets published after 1914

b recent and contemporary drama, fiction and poetry written for young people and adults

c drama, fiction and poetry by major writers from different cultures and traditions.

Non-fiction and non-literary texts

9 The range should include:

a literary non-fiction

b print and ICT-based information and reference texts

c media and moving image texts [for example, newspapers, magazines, advertisements, television, films, videos].

Examples of major playwrights
William Congreve, Oliver Goldsmith, Christopher Marlowe, Sean O'Casey, Harold Pinter, J B Priestley, Peter Shaffer, G B Shaw, R B Sheridan, Oscar Wilde.

List of major writers published before 1914 (see requirement 8a iii on page 35)
Jane Austen, Charlotte Brontë, Emily Brontë, John Bunyan, Wilkie Collins, Joseph Conrad, Daniel Defoe, Charles Dickens, Arthur Conan Doyle, George Eliot, Henry Fielding, Elizabeth Gaskell, Thomas Hardy, Henry James, Mary Shelley, Robert Louis Stevenson, Jonathan Swift, Anthony Trollope, H G Wells.

Examples of fiction by major writers after 1914
E M Forster, William Golding, Graham Greene, Aldous Huxley, James Joyce, D H Lawrence, Katherine Mansfield, George Orwell, Muriel Spark, William Trevor, Evelyn Waugh.

List of major poets published before 1914 (see requirement 8a v on page 35)
Matthew Arnold, Elizabeth Barrett Browning, William Blake, Emily Brontë, Robert Browning, Robert Burns, Lord Byron, Geoffrey Chaucer, John Clare, Samuel Taylor Coleridge, John Donne, John Dryden, Thomas Gray, George Herbert, Robert Herrick, Gerard Manley Hopkins, John Keats, Andrew Marvell, John Milton, Alexander Pope, Christina Rossetti, William Shakespeare (sonnets), Percy Bysshe Shelley, Edmund Spenser, Alfred Lord Tennyson, Henry Vaughan, William Wordsworth, Sir Thomas Wyatt.

Examples of major poets after 1914
W H Auden, Gillian Clarke, Keith Douglas, T S Eliot, U A Fanthorpe, Thomas Hardy, Seamus Heaney, Ted Hughes, Elizabeth Jennings, Philip Larkin, Wilfred Owen, Sylvia Plath, Stevie Smith, Edward Thomas, R S Thomas, W B Yeats.

Examples of recent and contemporary drama, fiction and poetry
Drama: Alan Ayckbourn, Samuel Beckett, Alan Bennett, Robert Bolt, Brian Friel, Willis Hall, David Hare, Willie Russell, R C Sherriff, Arnold Wesker.

Fiction: J G Ballard, Berlie Doherty, Susan Hill, Laurie Lee, Joan Lingard, Bill Naughton, Alan Sillitoe, Mildred Taylor, Robert Westall.

Poetry: Simon Armitage, James Berry, Douglas Dunn, Liz Lochhead, Adrian Mitchell, Edwin Muir, Grace Nichols, Jo Shapcott.

Examples of drama, fiction and poetry by major writers from different cultures and traditions
Drama: Athol Fugard, Arthur Miller, Wole Soyinka, Tennessee Williams.

Fiction: Chinua Achebe, Maya Angelou, Willa Cather, Anita Desai, Nadine Gordimer, Ernest Hemingway, H H Richardson, Doris Lessing, R K Narayan, John Steinbeck, Ngugi wa Thiong'o.

Poetry: E K Brathwaite, Emily Dickinson, Robert Frost, Robert Lowell, Les Murray, Rabindranath Tagore, Derek Walcott.

Examples of non-fiction and non-literary texts
Personal record and viewpoints on society: Peter Ackroyd, James Baldwin, John Berger, James Boswell, Vera Brittain, Lord Byron, William Cobbett, Gerald Durrell, Robert Graves, Samuel Johnson, Laurie Lee, Samuel Pepys, Flora Thompson, Beatrice Webb, Dorothy Wordsworth.

Travel writing: Jan Morris, Freya Stark, Laurens Van Der Post.

Reportage: James Cameron, Winston Churchill, Alistair Cooke, Dilys Powell.

The natural world: David Attenborough, Rachel Carson, Charles Darwin, Steve Jones.

En3 Writing

Knowledge, skills and understanding

Composition

1   Pupils should be taught to draw on their reading and knowledge of linguistic and literary forms when composing their writing. Pupils should be taught to:

Writing to imagine, explore, entertain

a   draw on their experience of good fiction, of different poetic forms and of reading, watching and performing in plays

b   use imaginative vocabulary and varied linguistic and literary techniques

c   exploit choice of language and structure to achieve particular effects and appeal to the reader

d   use a range of techniques and different ways of organising and structuring material to convey ideas, themes and characters

Writing to inform, explain, describe

e   form sentences and paragraphs that express connections between information and ideas precisely [for example, cause and effect, comparison]

f   use formal and impersonal language and concise expression

g   consider what the reader needs to know and include relevant details

h   present material clearly, using appropriate layout, illustrations and organisation

Writing to persuade, argue, advise

i   develop logical arguments and cite evidence

j   use persuasive techniques and rhetorical devices

k   anticipate reader reaction, counter opposing views and use language to gain attention and sustain interest

Writing to analyse, review, comment

l   reflect on the nature and significance of the subject matter

m   form their own view, taking into account a range of evidence and opinions

n   organise their ideas and information, distinguishing between analysis and comment

o   take account of how well the reader knows the topic.

Planning and drafting

2   To improve and sustain their writing, pupils should be taught to:

a   plan, draft, redraft and proofread their work on paper and on screen

b   judge the extent to which any or all of these processes are needed in specific pieces of writing

c   analyse critically their own and others' writing.

Writing: during key stages 3 and 4 pupils develop confidence in writing for a range of purposes. They develop their own distinctive styles and recognise the importance of writing with commitment and vitality. They learn to write correctly, using different formats, layouts and ways of presenting their work.

Note for 1d
The variety of narrative structures includes the use of words, sound and images.

1h → ICT opportunity
Pupils could make choices of font style and size and whether to use bold, italics or bullets in presenting their work.

Note for 2a
Planning and revising can be done simultaneously when working on screen.

Note for 4e

Using spellcheckers involves understanding both their uses and their limitations.

5c → ICT opportunity

Pupils could use a variety of ways to present their work, including using pictures and moving images as well as print.

Punctuation

3   Pupils should be taught to use the full range of punctuation marks correctly to signal sentence structure, and to help the reader.

Spelling

4   Pupils should be taught to:

a   increase their knowledge of regular patterns of spelling, word families, roots of words and derivations, including stem, prefix, suffix, inflection

b   apply their knowledge of word formation

c   spell increasingly complex polysyllabic words that do not conform to regular patterns

d   check their spelling for errors and use a dictionary when necessary

e   use different kinds of dictionary, thesaurus and spellchecker.

Handwriting and presentation

5   Pupils should be taught to write with fluency and, when required, speed. In presenting final polished work, pupils should be taught to:

a   ensure that work is neat and clear

b   write legibly, if their work is handwritten

c   make full use of different presentational devices where appropriate.

Standard English

6   Pupils should be taught about the variations in written standard English and how they differ from spoken language, and to distinguish varying degrees of formality, selecting appropriately for a task.

Language structure

7   Pupils should be taught the principles of sentence grammar and whole-text cohesion and use this knowledge in their writing. They should be taught:

a   word classes or parts of speech and their grammatical functions

b   the structure of phrases and clauses and how they can be combined to make complex sentences [for example, coordination and subordination]

c   paragraph structure and how to form different types of paragraph

d   the structure of whole texts, including cohesion, openings and conclusions in different types of writing [for example, through the use of verb tenses, reference chains]

e   the use of appropriate grammatical terminology to reflect on the meaning and clarity of individual sentences [for example, nouns, verbs, adjectives, prepositions, conjunctions, articles].

Breadth of study

8   During the key stage, pupils should be taught the **Knowledge, skills and understanding** through addressing the following range of purposes, readers and forms of writing.

9   The range of purposes for writing should include:

a   to imagine, explore and entertain, focusing on creative, aesthetic and literary uses of language. The forms for such writing should be drawn from different kinds of stories, poems, playscripts, autobiographies, screenplays, diaries

b   to inform, explain and describe, focusing on conveying information and ideas clearly. The forms for such writing should be drawn from memos, minutes, accounts, information leaflets, prospectuses, plans, records, summaries

c   to persuade, argue and advise, focusing on presenting a case and influencing the reader. The forms for such writing should be drawn from brochures, advertisements, editorials, articles and letters conveying opinions, campaign literature, polemical essays

d   to analyse, review and comment, focusing on considered and evaluative views of ideas, texts and issues. The forms for such writing should be drawn from reviews, commentaries, articles, essays, reports.

10   Pupils should also be taught to use writing for thinking and learning [for example, for hypothesising, paraphrasing, summarising, noting].

11   The range of readers for writing should include specific, known readers, a large, unknown readership and the pupils themselves.

Note for 9

Written texts are shaped by choices of purpose, form and reader. These elements are interdependent so that, for example, forms are adapted to the writer's aim and the intended reader.

General teaching requirements

Inclusion: providing effective learning opportunities for all pupils

Schools have a responsibility to provide a broad and balanced curriculum for all pupils. The National Curriculum is the starting point for planning a school curriculum that meets the specific needs of individuals and groups of pupils. This statutory inclusion statement on providing effective learning opportunities for all pupils outlines how teachers can modify, as necessary, the National Curriculum programmes of study to provide all pupils with relevant and appropriately challenging work at each key stage. It sets out three principles that are essential to developing a more inclusive curriculum:

A Setting suitable learning challenges

B Responding to pupils' diverse learning needs

C Overcoming potential barriers to learning and assessment for individuals and groups of pupils.

Applying these principles should keep to a minimum the need for aspects of the National Curriculum to be disapplied for a pupil.

Schools are able to provide other curricular opportunities outside the National Curriculum to meet the needs of individuals or groups of pupils such as speech and language therapy and mobility training.

Three principles for inclusion

In planning and teaching the National Curriculum, teachers are required to have due regard to the following principles.

A Setting suitable learning challenges

1 Teachers should aim to give every pupil the opportunity to experience success in learning and to achieve as high a standard as possible. The National Curriculum programmes of study set out what most pupils should be taught at each key stage – but teachers should teach the knowledge, skills and understanding in ways that suit their pupils' abilities. This may mean choosing knowledge, skills and understanding from earlier or later key stages so that individual pupils can make progress and show what they can achieve. Where it is appropriate for pupils to make extensive use of content from an earlier key stage, there may not be time to teach all aspects of the age-related programmes of study. A similarly flexible approach will be needed to take account of any gaps in pupils' learning resulting from missed or interrupted schooling [for example, that may be experienced by travellers, refugees, those in care or those with long-term medical conditions, including pupils with neurological problems, such as head injuries, and those with degenerative conditions].

2   For pupils whose attainments fall significantly below the expected levels at a particular key stage, a much greater degree of differentiation will be necessary. In these circumstances, teachers may need to use the content of the programmes of study as a resource or to provide a context, in planning learning appropriate to the age and requirements of their pupils.[1]

3   For pupils whose attainments significantly exceed the expected level of attainment within one or more subjects during a particular key stage, teachers will need to plan suitably challenging work. As well as drawing on materials from later key stages or higher levels of study, teachers may plan further differentiation by extending the breadth and depth of study within individual subjects or by planning work which draws on the content of different subjects.[2]

B   Responding to pupils' diverse learning needs

1   When planning, teachers should set high expectations and provide opportunities for all pupils to achieve, including boys and girls, pupils with special educational needs, pupils with disabilities, pupils from all social and cultural backgrounds, pupils of different ethnic groups including travellers, refugees and asylum seekers, and those from diverse linguistic backgrounds. Teachers need to be aware that pupils bring to school different experiences, interests and strengths which will influence the way in which they learn. Teachers should plan their approaches to teaching and learning so that all pupils can take part in lessons fully and effectively.

2   To ensure that they meet the full range of pupils' needs, teachers should be aware of the requirements of the equal opportunities legislation that covers race, gender and disability.[3]

3   Teachers should take specific action to respond to pupils' diverse needs by:
    a   creating effective learning environments
    b   securing their motivation and concentration
    c   providing equality of opportunity through teaching approaches
    d   using appropriate assessment approaches
    e   setting targets for learning.

Examples for B/3a – creating effective learning environments
Teachers create effective learning environments in which:
■   the contribution of all pupils is valued
■   all pupils can feel secure and are able to contribute appropriately
■   stereotypical views are challenged and pupils learn to appreciate and view positively differences in others, whether arising from race, gender, ability or disability

---

[1] Teachers may find QCA's guidance on planning work for pupils with learning difficulties a helpful companion to the programmes of study.
[2] Teachers may find QCA's guidance on meeting the requirements of gifted and talented pupils a helpful companion to the programmes of study.
[3] The Sex Discrimination Act 1975, the Race Relations Act 1976, the Disability Discrimination Act 1995.

- pupils learn to take responsibility for their actions and behaviours both in school and in the wider community
- all forms of bullying and harassment, including racial harassment, are challenged
- pupils are enabled to participate safely in clothing appropriate to their religious beliefs, particularly in subjects such as science, design and technology and physical education.

Examples for B/3b – securing motivation and concentration

Teachers secure pupils' motivation and concentration by:

- using teaching approaches appropriate to different learning styles
- using, where appropriate, a range of organisational approaches, such as setting, grouping or individual work, to ensure that learning needs are properly addressed
- varying subject content and presentation so that this matches their learning needs
- planning work which builds on their interests and cultural experiences
- planning appropriately challenging work for those whose ability and understanding are in advance of their language skills
- using materials which reflect social and cultural diversity and provide positive images of race, gender and disability
- planning and monitoring the pace of work so that they all have a chance to learn effectively and achieve success
- taking action to maintain interest and continuity of learning for pupils who may be absent for extended periods of time.

Examples for B/3c – providing equality of opportunity

Teaching approaches that provide equality of opportunity include:

- ensuring that boys and girls are able to participate in the same curriculum, particularly in science, design and technology and physical education
- taking account of the interests and concerns of boys and girls by using a range of activities and contexts for work and allowing a variety of interpretations and outcomes, particularly in English, science, design and technology, ICT, art and design, music and physical education
- avoiding gender stereotyping when organising pupils into groups, assigning them to activities or arranging access to equipment, particularly in science, design and technology, ICT, music and physical education
- taking account of pupils' specific religious or cultural beliefs relating to the representation of ideas or experiences or to the use of particular types of equipment, particularly in science, design and technology, ICT and art and design
- enabling the fullest possible participation of pupils with disabilities or particular medical needs in all subjects, offering positive role models and making provision, where necessary, to facilitate access to activities with appropriate support, aids or adaptations. (See **Overcoming potential barriers to learning and assessment for individuals and groups of pupils.**)

Examples for B/3d – using appropriate assessment approaches
Teachers use appropriate assessment approaches that:

- allow for different learning styles and ensure that pupils are given the chance and encouragement to demonstrate their competence and attainment through appropriate means
- are familiar to the pupils and for which they have been adequately prepared
- use materials which are free from discrimination and stereotyping in any form
- provide clear and unambiguous feedback to pupils to aid further learning.

Examples for B/3e – setting targets for learning
Teachers set targets for learning that:

- build on pupils' knowledge, experiences, interests and strengths to improve areas of weakness and demonstrate progression over time
- are attainable and yet challenging and help pupils to develop their self-esteem and confidence in their ability to learn.

C Overcoming potential barriers to learning and assessment for individuals and groups of pupils

A minority of pupils will have particular learning and assessment requirements which go beyond the provisions described in sections A and B and, if not addressed, could create barriers to learning. These requirements are likely to arise as a consequence of a pupil having a special educational need or disability or may be linked to a pupil's progress in learning English as an additional language.

1   Teachers must take account of these requirements and make provision, where necessary, to support individuals or groups of pupils to enable them to participate effectively in the curriculum and assessment activities. During end of key stage assessments, teachers should bear in mind that special arrangements are available to support individual pupils.

Pupils with special educational needs

2   Curriculum planning and assessment for pupils with special educational needs must take account of the type and extent of the difficulty experienced by the pupil. Teachers will encounter a wide range of pupils with special educational needs, some of whom will also have disabilities (see paragraphs C/4 and C/5). In many cases, the action necessary to respond to an individual's requirements for curriculum access will be met through greater differentiation of tasks and materials, consistent with school-based intervention as set out in the SEN Code of Practice. A smaller number of pupils may need access to specialist equipment and approaches or to alternative or adapted activities, consistent with school-based intervention augmented by advice and support from external specialists as described in the SEN Code of Practice, or, in exceptional circumstances, with a statement of special educational need.

Teachers should, where appropriate, work closely with representatives of other agencies who may be supporting the pupil.

3   Teachers should take specific action to provide access to learning for pupils with special educational needs by:

   a   providing for pupils who need help with communication, language and literacy

   b   planning, where necessary, to develop pupils' understanding through the use of all available senses and experiences

   c   planning for pupils' full participation in learning and in physical and practical activities

   d   helping pupils to manage their behaviour, to take part in learning effectively and safely, and, at key stage 4, to prepare for work

   e   helping individuals to manage their emotions, particularly trauma or stress, and to take part in learning.

Examples for C/3a – helping with communication, language and literacy
Teachers provide for pupils who need help with communication, language and literacy through:

- using texts that pupils can read and understand
- using visual and written materials in different formats, including large print, symbol text and Braille
- using ICT, other technological aids and taped materials
- using alternative and augmentative communication, including signs and symbols
- using translators, communicators and amanuenses.

Examples for C/3b – developing understanding
Teachers develop pupils' understanding through the use of all available senses and experiences, by:

- using materials and resources that pupils can access through sight, touch, sound, taste or smell
- using word descriptions and other stimuli to make up for a lack of first-hand experiences
- using ICT, visual and other materials to increase pupils' knowledge of the wider world
- encouraging pupils to take part in everyday activities such as play, drama, class visits and exploring the environment.

Examples for C/3c – planning for full participation
Teachers plan for pupils' full participation in learning and in physical and practical activities through:

- using specialist aids and equipment
- providing support from adults or peers when needed
- adapting tasks or environments
- providing alternative activities, where necessary.

Examples for C/3d – managing behaviour

Teachers help pupils to manage their behaviour, take part in learning effectively and safely, and, at key stage 4, prepare for work by:

- setting realistic demands and stating them explicitly
- using positive behaviour management, including a clear structure of rewards and sanctions
- giving pupils every chance and encouragement to develop the skills they need to work well with a partner or a group
- teaching pupils to value and respect the contribution of others
- encouraging and teaching independent working skills
- teaching essential safety rules.

Examples for C/3e – managing emotions

Teachers help individuals manage their emotions and take part in learning through:

- identifying aspects of learning in which the pupil will engage and plan short-term, easily achievable goals in selected activities
- providing positive feedback to reinforce and encourage learning and build self-esteem
- selecting tasks and materials sensitively to avoid unnecessary stress for the pupil
- creating a supportive learning environment in which the pupil feels safe and is able to engage with learning
- allowing time for the pupil to engage with learning and gradually increasing the range of activities and demands.

Pupils with disabilities

4   Not all pupils with disabilities will necessarily have special educational needs. Many pupils with disabilities learn alongside their peers with little need for additional resources beyond the aids which they use as part of their daily life, such as a wheelchair, a hearing aid or equipment to aid vision. Teachers must take action, however, in their planning to ensure that these pupils are enabled to participate as fully and effectively as possible within the National Curriculum and the statutory assessment arrangements. Potential areas of difficulty should be identified and addressed at the outset of work, without recourse to the formal provisions for disapplication.

5   Teachers should take specific action to enable the effective participation of pupils with disabilities by:

a   planning appropriate amounts of time to allow for the satisfactory completion of tasks

b   planning opportunities, where necessary, for the development of skills in practical aspects of the curriculum

c   identifying aspects of programmes of study and attainment targets that may present specific difficulties for individuals.

Examples for C/5a – planning to complete tasks

Teachers plan appropriate amounts of time to allow pupils to complete tasks satisfactorily through:

- taking account of the very slow pace at which some pupils will be able to record work, either manually or with specialist equipment, and of the physical effort required
- being aware of the high levels of concentration necessary for some pupils when following or interpreting text or graphics, particularly when using vision aids or tactile methods, and of the tiredness which may result
- allocating sufficient time, opportunity and access to equipment for pupils to gain information through experimental work and detailed observation, including the use of microscopes
- being aware of the effort required by some pupils to follow oral work, whether through use of residual hearing, lip reading or a signer, and of the tiredness or loss of concentration which may occur.

Examples for C/5b – developing skills in practical aspects

Teachers create opportunities for the development of skills in practical aspects of the curriculum through:

- providing adapted, modified or alternative activities or approaches to learning in physical education and ensuring that these have integrity and equivalence to the National Curriculum and enable pupils to make appropriate progress
- providing alternative or adapted activities in science, art and design and design and technology for pupils who are unable to manipulate tools, equipment or materials or who may be allergic to certain types of materials
- ensuring that all pupils can be included and participate safely in geography fieldwork, local studies and visits to museums, historic buildings and sites.

Examples for C/5c – overcoming specific difficulties

Teachers overcome specific difficulties for individuals presented by aspects of the programmes of study and attainment targets through:

- using approaches to enable hearing impaired pupils to learn about sound in science and music
- helping visually impaired pupils to learn about light in science, to access maps and visual resources in geography and to evaluate different products in design and technology and images in art and design
- providing opportunities for pupils to develop strength in depth where they cannot meet the particular requirements of a subject, such as the visual requirements in art and design and the singing requirements in music
- discounting these aspects in appropriate individual cases when required to make a judgement against level descriptions.

Pupils who are learning English as an additional language

6 Pupils for whom English is an additional language have diverse needs in terms of support necessary in English language learning. Planning should take account of such factors as the pupil's age, length of time in this country, previous educational experience and skills in other languages. Careful monitoring of each pupil's progress in the acquisition of English language skills and of subject knowledge and understanding will be necessary to confirm that no learning difficulties are present.

7 The ability of pupils for whom English is an additional language to take part in the National Curriculum may be ahead of their communication skills in English. Teachers should plan learning opportunities to help pupils develop their English and should aim to provide the support pupils need to take part in all subject areas.

8 Teachers should take specific action to help pupils who are learning English as an additional language by:
   a developing their spoken and written English
   b ensuring access to the curriculum and to assessment.

Examples for C/8a – developing spoken and written English

Teachers develop pupils' spoken and written English through:
- ensuring that vocabulary work covers both the technical and everyday meaning of key words, metaphors and idioms
- explaining clearly how speaking and writing in English are structured to achieve different purposes, across a range of subjects
- providing a variety of reading material [for example, pupils' own work, the media, ICT, literature, reference books] that highlight the different ways English is used, especially those that help pupils to understand society and culture
- ensuring that there are effective opportunities for talk and that talk is used to support writing in all subjects
- where appropriate, encouraging pupils to transfer their knowledge, skills and understanding of one language to another, pointing out similarities and differences between languages
- building on pupils' experiences of language at home and in the wider community, so that their developing uses of English and other languages support one another.

Examples for C/8b – ensuring access

Teachers make sure pupils have access to the curriculum and to assessment through:
- using accessible texts and materials that suit pupils' ages and levels of learning
- providing support by using ICT or video or audio materials, dictionaries and translators, readers and amanuenses
- using home or first language, where appropriate.

Additional information for English

Teachers may find the following additional information helpful when implementing the statutory inclusion statement **Providing effective learning opportunities for all pupils**. Teachers need to consider the full requirements of the inclusion statement when planning for individuals or groups of pupils. Specific references to English are included in the examples for B/3c and C/8a.

To overcome any potential barriers to learning in English, some pupils may require:

- support in overcoming specific difficulties in learning which result in an uneven profile across the attainment targets. They will require help to improve areas of weakness and strategies for managing specific difficulties
- opportunities to meet the demands for speaking and listening and other oral activities through the use of alternative communication systems, to compensate for difficulties in using spoken language
- opportunities to learn and develop alternative methods of recording, such as ICT, to compensate for difficulties with handwriting, to enable them to demonstrate their wider writing skills
- opportunities to learn and develop tactile methods of interpreting written information, to overcome difficulties in managing visual information.

In assessment:

- where pupils use alternative communication systems, judgements should be made against the level descriptions for speaking and listening. It will be necessary to note any demands that are not met, such as the awareness and use of standard English
- for pupils with disabilities who are unable to write by hand, the handwriting requirement of the writing attainment target will not be applicable
- for pupils using tactile methods, the assessment of reading will be through the use of materials of equivalent demand presented in the appropriate medium.

Use of language across the curriculum

1   Pupils should be taught in all subjects to express themselves correctly and appropriately and to read accurately and with understanding. Since standard English, spoken and written, is the predominant language in which knowledge and skills are taught and learned, pupils should be taught to recognise and use standard English.

Writing

2   In writing, pupils should be taught to use correct spelling and punctuation and follow grammatical conventions. They should also be taught to organise their writing in logical and coherent forms.

Speaking

3   In speaking, pupils should be taught to use language precisely and cogently.

Listening

4   Pupils should be taught to listen to others, and to respond and build on their ideas and views constructively.

Reading

5   In reading, pupils should be taught strategies to help them read with understanding, to locate and use information, to follow a process or argument and summarise, and to synthesise and adapt what they learn from their reading.

6   Pupils should be taught the technical and specialist vocabulary of subjects and how to use and spell these words. They should also be taught to use the patterns of language vital to understanding and expression in different subjects. These include the construction of sentences, paragraphs and texts that are often used in a subject [for example, language to express causality, chronology, logic, exploration, hypothesis, comparison, and how to ask questions and develop arguments].

Use of information and communication technology across the curriculum

1   Pupils should be given opportunities[1] to apply and develop their ICT capability through the use of ICT tools to support their learning in all subjects (with the exception of physical education at key stages 1 and 2).

2   Pupils should be given opportunities to support their work by being taught to:
    a   find things out from a variety of sources, selecting and synthesising the information to meet their needs and developing an ability to question its accuracy, bias and plausibility
    b   develop their ideas using ICT tools to amend and refine their work and enhance its quality and accuracy
    c   exchange and share information, both directly and through electronic media
    d   review, modify and evaluate their work, reflecting critically on its quality, as it progresses.

[1] At key stage 1, there are no statutory requirements to teach the use of ICT in the programmes of study for the non-core foundation subjects. Teachers should use their judgement to decide where it is appropriate to teach the use of ICT across these subjects at key stage 1. At other key stages, there are statutory requirements to use ICT in all subjects, except physical education.

The attainment targets for English

About the attainment targets

An attainment target sets out the 'knowledge, skills and understanding that pupils of different abilities and maturities are expected to have by the end of each key stage'[1]. Except in the case of citizenship[2], attainment targets consist of eight level descriptions of increasing difficulty, plus a description for exceptional performance above level 8. Each level description describes the types and range of performance that pupils working at that level should characteristically demonstrate.

The level descriptions provide the basis for making judgements about pupils' performance at the end of key stages 1, 2 and 3. At key stage 4, national qualifications are the main means of assessing attainment in English.

Range of levels within which the great majority of pupils are expected to work		Expected attainment for the majority of pupils at the end of the key stage	
Key stage 1	**1–3**	at age 7	**2**
Key stage 2	**2–5**	at age 11	**4**
Key stage 3	**3–7**	at age 14	**5/6**[3]

Assessing attainment at the end of a key stage

In deciding on a pupil's level of attainment at the end of a key stage, teachers should judge which description best fits the pupil's performance. When doing so, each description should be considered alongside descriptions for adjacent levels.

Arrangements for statutory assessment at the end of each key stage are set out in detail in QCA's annual booklets about assessment and reporting arrangements.

[1] As defined by the Education Act 1996, section 353a.
[2] In citizenship, expected performance for the majority of pupils at the end of key stages 3 and 4 is set out in end of key stage descriptions.
[3] Including modern foreign languages.

Attainment target 2: reading

Level 1

Pupils recognise familiar words in simple texts. They use their knowledge of letters and sound–symbol relationships in order to read words and to establish meaning when reading aloud. In these activities they sometimes require support. They express their response to poems, stories and non-fiction by identifying aspects they like.

Level 2

Pupils' reading of simple texts shows understanding and is generally accurate. They express opinions about major events or ideas in stories, poems and non-fiction. They use more than one strategy, such as phonic, graphic, syntactic and contextual, in reading unfamiliar words and establishing meaning.

Level 3

Pupils read a range of texts fluently and accurately. They read independently, using strategies appropriately to establish meaning. In responding to fiction and non-fiction they show understanding of the main points and express preferences. They use their knowledge of the alphabet to locate books and find information.

Level 4

In responding to a range of texts, pupils show understanding of significant ideas, themes, events and characters, beginning to use inference and deduction. They refer to the text when explaining their views. They locate and use ideas and information.

Level 5

Pupils show understanding of a range of texts, selecting essential points and using inference and deduction where appropriate. In their responses, they identify key features, themes and characters and select sentences, phrases and relevant information to support their views. They retrieve and collate information from a range of sources.

Level 6

In reading and discussing a range of texts, pupils identify different layers of meaning and comment on their significance and effect. They give personal responses to literary texts, referring to aspects of language, structure and themes in justifying their views. They summarise a range of information from different sources.

Level 7

Pupils show understanding of the ways in which meaning and information are conveyed in a range of texts. They articulate personal and critical responses to poems, plays and novels, showing awareness of their thematic, structural and linguistic features. They select and synthesise a range of information from a variety of sources.

Level 8

Pupils' response is shown in their appreciation of, and comment on, a range of texts, and they evaluate how authors achieve their effects through the use of linguistic, structural and presentational devices. They select and analyse information and ideas, and comment on how these are conveyed in different texts.

Exceptional performance

Pupils confidently sustain their responses to a demanding range of texts, developing their ideas and referring in detail to aspects of language, structure and presentation. They make apt and careful comparison between texts, including consideration of audience, purpose and form. They identify and analyse argument, opinion and alternative interpretations, making cross-references where appropriate.

Level 5

Pupils talk and listen confidently in a wide range of contexts, including some that are of a formal nature. Their talk engages the interest of the listener as they begin to vary their expression and vocabulary. In discussion, they pay close attention to what others say, ask questions to develop ideas and make contributions that take account of others' views. They begin to use standard English in formal situations.

Level 6

Pupils adapt their talk to the demands of different contexts with increasing confidence. Their talk engages the interest of the listener through the variety of its vocabulary and expression. Pupils take an active part in discussion, showing understanding of ideas and sensitivity to others. They are usually fluent in their use of standard English in formal situations.

Level 7

Pupils are confident in matching their talk to the demands of different contexts. They use vocabulary precisely and organise their talk to communicate clearly. In discussion, pupils make significant contributions, evaluating others' ideas and varying how and when they participate. They show confident use of standard English in situations that require it.

Level 8

Pupils maintain and develop their talk purposefully in a range of contexts. They structure what they say clearly, using apt vocabulary and appropriate intonation and emphasis. They make a range of contributions which show that they have listened perceptively and are sensitive to the development of discussion. They show confident use of standard English in a range of situations, adapting as necessary.

Exceptional performance

Pupils select and use structures, styles and registers appropriately in a range of contexts, varying their vocabulary and expression confidently for a range of purposes. They initiate and sustain discussion through the sensitive use of a variety of contributions. They take a leading role in discussion and listen with concentration and understanding to varied and complex speech. They show assured and fluent use of standard English in a range of situations and for a variety of purposes.

Attainment target 1: speaking and listening

Level 1

Pupils talk about matters of immediate interest. They listen to others and usually respond appropriately. They convey simple meanings to a range of listeners, speaking audibly, and begin to extend their ideas or accounts by providing some detail.

Level 2

Pupils begin to show confidence in talking and listening, particularly where the topics interest them. On occasions, they show awareness of the needs of the listener by including relevant detail. In developing and explaining their ideas they speak clearly and use a growing vocabulary. They usually listen carefully and respond with increasing appropriateness to what others say. They are beginning to be aware that in some situations a more formal vocabulary and tone of voice are used.

Level 3

Pupils talk and listen confidently in different contexts, exploring and communicating ideas. In discussion, they show understanding of the main points. Through relevant comments and questions, they show they have listened carefully. They begin to adapt what they say to the needs of the listener, varying the use of vocabulary and the level of detail. They are beginning to be aware of standard English and when it is used.

Level 4

Pupils talk and listen with confidence in an increasing range of contexts. Their talk is adapted to the purpose: developing ideas thoughtfully, describing events and conveying their opinions clearly. In discussion, they listen carefully, making contributions and asking questions that are responsive to others' ideas and views. They use appropriately some of the features of standard English vocabulary and grammar.

Acknowledgements

About the work used in this document
The artwork and photographs used in this book are the result of a national selection organised by QCA and the Design Council. We would like to thank all 3,108 pupils who took part and especially the following pupils and schools whose work has been used throughout the National Curriculum.

Pupils Frankie Allen, Sarah Anderson, Naomi Ball, Kristina Battleday, Ashley Boyle, Martin Broom, Katie Brown, Alex Bryant, Tania Burnett, Elizabeth Burrows, Caitie Calloway, Kavandeep Chahal, Donna Clarke, Leah Cliffe, Megan Coombs, Andrew Cornford, Samantha Davidoff, Jodie Evans, Holly Fowler, Rachel Fort, Christopher Fort, Hannah Foster, Ruth Fry, Nicholas Furlonge, Tasleem Ghanchi, Rebecca Goodwin, Megan Goodwin, Joanna Gray, Alisha Grazette, Emma Habbeshon, Zoe Hall, Kay Hampshire, Jessica Harris, Aimee Howard, Amy Hurst, Katherine Hymers, Safwan Ismael, Tamaszina Jacobs-Abiola, Tomi Johnson, Richard Jones, Bruno Jones, Thomas Kelleher, Sophie Lambert, Gareth Lloyd, Ope Majekodunmi, Sophie Manchester, Alex Massie, Amy McNair, Dale Meachen, Katherine Mills, Rebecca Moore, Andrew Morgan, Amber Murrell, Sally O'Connor, Rosie O'Reilly, Antonia Pain, Daniel Pamment, Jennie Plant, Christopher Prest, Megan Ramsay, Alice Ross, David Rowles, Amy Sandford, Zeba Saudagar, Nathan Scarfe, Daniel Scully, Bilal Shakoor, Sandeep Sharma, Morrad Siyahla, Daryl Smith, Catriona Statham, Scott Taylor, Amy Thornton, Jessica Tidmarsh, Alix Tinkler, Lucy Titford, Marion Tulloch, Charlotte Ward, Kaltuun Warsame, Emily Webb, Bradley West, Daniel Wilkinson, Soriah Williams, Susan Williamson, Helen Williamson, Charlotte Windmill, Ryan Wollan, Olivia Wright.

Schools Adam's Grammar School, Almondbury Junior School, Bishops Castle Community College, Bolton Brow Junior and Infant School, Boxford C of E Voluntary Controlled Primary School, Bugbrooke School, Cantell School, Charnwood Primary School, Cheselbourne County First School, Chester Catholic High School, Dales Infant School, Deanery C of E High School, Driffield C of E Infants' School, Dursley Primary School, Fourfields County Primary School, Furze Infants School, Gosforth High School, Grahame Park Junior School, Green Park Combined School, Gusford Community Primary School, Hartshill School, Headington School, Holyport Manor School, Jersey College for Girls Preparatory School, King Edward VI School, King James's School, Kingsway Junior School, Knutsford High School, Leiston Primary School, Maltby Manor Infant School, Mullion Comprehensive School, North Marston C of E First School, Norton Hill School, Penglais School, Priory Secondary School, Redknock School, Richard Whittington Primary School, Ringwood School, Sarah Bonnell School, Sedgemoor Manor Infants School, Selly Park Technology College for Girls, Southwark Infant School, St Albans High School for Girls, St Denys C of E Infant School, St Helen's C of E (Aided) Primary School, St John's Infants School, St Joseph's RC Infant School, St Laurence School, St Mary Magdalene School, St Matthews C of E Aided Primary School, St Michael's C of E School, St Saviour's and St Olave's School, St Thomas The Martyr C of E Primary School, Sawtry Community College, The Duchess's High School, Tideway School, Torfield School, Trinity C of E Primary School, Upper Poppleton School, Walton High School.

QCA and the Design Council would also like to thank the figures from public life who contributed their ideas about the value of each curriculum subject.

Attainment target 3: writing

Level 1

Pupils' writing communicates meaning through simple words and phrases. In their reading or their writing, pupils begin to show awareness of how full stops are used. Letters are usually clearly shaped and correctly orientated.

Level 2

Pupils' writing communicates meaning in both narrative and non-narrative forms, using appropriate and interesting vocabulary, and showing some awareness of the reader. Ideas are developed in a sequence of sentences, sometimes demarcated by capital letters and full stops. Simple, monosyllabic words are usually spelt correctly, and where there are inaccuracies the alternative is phonetically plausible. In handwriting, letters are accurately formed and consistent in size.

Level 3

Pupils' writing is often organised, imaginative and clear. The main features of different forms of writing are used appropriately, beginning to be adapted to different readers. Sequences of sentences extend ideas logically and words are chosen for variety and interest. The basic grammatical structure of sentences is usually correct. Spelling is usually accurate, including that of common, polysyllabic words. Punctuation to mark sentences – full stops, capital letters and question marks – is used accurately. Handwriting is joined and legible.

Level 4

Pupils' writing in a range of forms is lively and thoughtful. Ideas are often sustained and developed in interesting ways and organised appropriately for the purpose of the reader. Vocabulary choices are often adventurous and words are used for effect. Pupils are beginning to use grammatically complex sentences, extending meaning. Spelling, including that of polysyllabic words that conform to regular patterns, is generally accurate. Full stops, capital letters and question marks are used correctly, and pupils are beginning to use punctuation within the sentence. Handwriting style is fluent, joined and legible.

Level 5

Pupils' writing is varied and interesting, conveying meaning clearly in a range of forms for different readers, using a more formal style where appropriate. Vocabulary choices are imaginative and words are used precisely. Simple and complex sentences are organised into paragraphs. Words with complex regular patterns are usually spelt correctly. A range of punctuation, including commas, apostrophes and inverted commas, is usually used accurately. Handwriting is joined, clear and fluent and, where appropriate, is adapted to a range of tasks.

Level 6

Pupils' writing often engages and sustains the reader's interest, showing some adaptation of style and register to different forms, including using an impersonal style where appropriate. Pupils use a range of sentence structures and varied vocabulary to create effects. Spelling is generally accurate, including that of irregular words. Handwriting is neat and legible. A range of punctuation is usually used correctly to clarify meaning, and ideas are organised into paragraphs.

Level 7

Pupils' writing is confident and shows appropriate choices of style in a range of forms. In narrative writing, characters and settings are developed and, in non-fiction, ideas are organised and coherent. Grammatical features and vocabulary are accurately and effectively used. Spelling is correct, including that of complex irregular words. Work is legible and attractively presented. Paragraphing and correct punctuation are used to make the sequence of events or ideas coherent and clear to the reader.

Level 8

Pupils' writing shows the selection of specific features or expressions to convey particular effects and to interest the reader. Narrative writing shows control of characters, events and settings, and shows variety in structure. Non-fiction writing is coherent and gives clear points of view. The use of vocabulary and grammar enables fine distinctions to be made or emphasis achieved. Writing shows a clear grasp of the use of punctuation and paragraphing.

Exceptional performance

Pupils' writing has shape and impact and shows control of a range of styles maintaining the interest of the reader throughout. Narratives use structure as well as vocabulary for a range of imaginative effects, and non-fiction is coherent, reasoned and persuasive. A variety of grammatical constructions and punctuation is used accurately and appropriately and with sensitivity. Paragraphs are well constructed and linked in order to clarify the organisation of the writing as a whole.